Teen Suicide

Perspectives on Mental Health

by Judith Peacock

Consultant:
Jackie Casey, JD
Executive Director
Suicide Awareness\Voices of Education (SA\VE)

LifeMatters
an imprint of Capstone Press
Mankato, Minnesota

LifeMatters Books are published by Capstone Press
PO Box 669 • 151 Good Counsel Drive • Mankato, Minnesota 56002
http://www.capstone-press.com

Printed in the United States of America

Library of Congress Cataloging-in-Publication Data
Peacock, Judith, 1942-
     Teen suicide / by Judith Peacock.
             p.   cm. — (Perspectives on mental health)
     Includes bibliographical references and index.
     Summary: Examines some of the causes of suicide among teenagers and discusses ways to recognize potential victims and prevent this tragedy.
     ISBN 0-7368-0436-6 (book) — ISBN 0-7368-0440-4 (series)
     1. Teenagers—Suicidal behavior—Juvenile literature. [1. Suicide.] I. Title. II. Series.
     RJ506.S9 P43 2000
     616.85′8445′00835—dc21   99-056215
                                               CIP

Staff Credits
Marta Fahrenz, editor; Adam Lazar, designer; Jodi Theisen, photo researcher

Photo Credits
Cover: ©Capstone Press/Adam Lazar
FPG International/©Dick Luria, 6; ©Michael Hart, 12; ©Ken Ross, 15; ©Jill Sabella, 19; ©Ron Chapple, 25; ©James Porto, 40
International Stock/©Don Romero, 35; ©Patrick Ramsey, 46
Photo Network/©H.B. Jenssen, 33; ©Esbin-Anderson, 48; ©Patrick Ramsey, 59
Unicorn Stock Photos/©Eric R. Berndt, 9; ©Tom McCarthy, 27; ©Karen Moisinger Mullen, 57
Uniphoto Picture Agency/©Stephen Whalen, 20; ©Jackson Smith, 36; ©Bob Daemmrich, 53

A 0 9 8 7 6 5 4 3 2 1

Table of Contents

Chapter Overview

Teen suicide in the United States and Canada is a growing problem. About 5,000 teens in the United States kill themselves each year. Hidden suicides could push this number even higher.

The number of teens who attempt suicide each year also is staggering.

The number one cause of suicide is untreated depression. Depression can be treated.

Most teens have thought about suicide at some point.

Suicide isn't an answer to a problem. It is the fatal symptom of a disease.

Chapter 1

The Facts About Teen Suicide

Suicide is a tragedy at any age. It is especially tragic when it happens to teens. Suicide is the act of taking one's own life. Teens who kill themselves miss the chance to fulfill their dreams. Sadly, more young people are killing themselves today than ever before.

It was a beautiful spring day.
Rick arrived home from school.

RICK, AGE 16

He went to the refrigerator and took out a carton of milk. Rick took a long, thirsty gulp. Then he put back the carton and headed for the basement.

In the basement, Rick found the key to his dad's gun cabinet. He unlocked the cabinet, took out a shotgun, and loaded it. Rick put the gun to his head and pulled the trigger.

A Growing Problem

About 5,000 teens kill themselves each year in the United States. Suicide is the second-leading cause of death for young people between ages 15 and 19. Accidents rank first.

The number of teen suicides has tripled since the 1950s. Suicide rates for children and teens between ages 10 and 14 have increased 120 percent since 1980. Research shows that the availability of guns is a significant factor in the increase of teen suicide. Guns are used in nearly two of three teen suicides.

White males have the highest suicide rate among teens. However, the suicide rate for African American males ages 15 to 19 has increased 165 percent since 1980. This is the largest increase for teens. African American males now have suicide rates almost as high as white males.

Why Are Teen Suicides Increasing?

No one is sure why more teens today are taking their own life. Some experts point to the rising divorce rate and breakdown of family life. Others point to problems in society such as more violence. Another reason given is the widespread use of alcohol and other drugs.

Many youth feel hopeless about the future. Today's teens face pressures unheard of 40 years ago. Such pressures in the life of a teen who has depression or some other mental illness can be fatal.

In Canada, suicide is the second most common killer of teens. Canada has the third highest suicide rate of developed nations.

Hidden Suicides

The number of teen suicides in the United States each year may be much higher than 5,000. Some teen deaths labeled as accidents really are suicides. For example, death from a drug overdose or a single car accident may be a suicide. These are hidden suicides. In some cases, it cannot be proven that the death was a suicide. In other cases, parents may want to hide the fact that their son or daughter died by suicide.

Teens also exhibit reckless actions that may be related to suicidal behavior. They may abuse alcohol or other drugs. They may have an eating disorder that destroys organs such as the heart or lungs. Often teens do not realize the danger of their actions. Statistics on teen suicide do not include hidden suicides or fatal, self-harming behavior.

Attempted Suicides

The number of teens who attempt suicide also is high. In surveys, about 14 percent of adolescents said that they had tried to kill themselves. The number probably is much higher. In an average high school classroom of 30 students, 3 or 4 students may have attempted suicide.

All suicide attempts must be taken seriously. Attempts that fail can have tragic and serious results. Suicide attempts may be the first signal that a teen has an illness such as depression.

Three to four times as many girls as boys attempt suicide. Girls are more likely to have depression, which is a risk factor for suicide. On the other hand, four times as many boys complete suicide.

Curtis seemed to have everything going for him. He

CURTIS, AGE 17

was cocaptain of the basketball team and vice president of his class. Curtis also felt angry, sad, and desperate, but he didn't know why.

Curtis tried to escape from his feelings by jumping off a railroad bridge. He was still alive when the police found him. They brought him to a hospital.

Curtis damaged his spinal cord. Now he spends his days in a wheelchair. He can't feed, dress, or bathe himself. He uses a special machine to speak. Curtis wishes he had told someone about his feelings. Maybe he wouldn't have tried to end his life.

Untreated Depression as a Cause

Untreated depression is the number one cause of teen suicide. Depression is an illness that affects about 12 percent of teens. People with depression have deep feelings of sadness and hopelessness that continue for more than two weeks.

Some types of depression include bipolar disorder (also known as manic depression), dysthymia, and seasonal affective disorder (SAD). People with bipolar disorder have extreme mood swings. They alternate between feeling very low and very high. Dysthymia is a form of mild to moderate depression. People with dysthymia are able to function in daily life. However, they do not seem to enjoy living. SAD is a type of major depression. Its episodes correspond to the seasons.

Depression can be treated and cured. Chapter 4 includes more information about depression.

Suicidal Thoughts

You may have had suicidal thoughts. You are not alone. Some studies show that about 60 percent of high school students say they have considered suicide. Experts suggest that everyone at some time will think about suicide.

Thoughts of suicide may cross your mind when things go badly. If these thoughts do not go away, you need to seek help right away. These feelings are symptoms, or signs, of diseases like depression. They can be treated. Suicide is never the answer.

Points to Consider

Do you know of a teen who took his or her own life? What were the circumstances?

In your opinion, what is the reason for the large number of teen suicides and attempted suicides?

Have you had thoughts of suicide? What did you do about them?

Chapter
Overview

No single reason explains why teens kill themselves.

Lack of experience and poor problem-solving skills contribute to teen suicide.

In general, teens who kill themselves want to escape overpowering problems and painful feelings.

A suicide trigger is an event that causes a teen to act on his or her suicidal thoughts.

Teen suicide attempts often reveal unrealistic views of death.

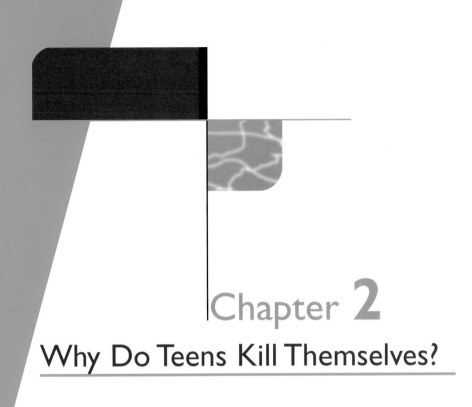

Chapter 2
Why Do Teens Kill Themselves?

Why do teens kill themselves? Young people seem to have everything to live for. What could be so wrong that a teen would want to take his or her own life?

A Permanent Solution to a Temporary Problem

There is no single cause for suicide. Every suicide is different. Sometimes the cause is never known. In general, teens choose suicide to solve problems that overwhelm them. They may want to escape a desperate situation. They may want to stop negative thoughts and feelings. Suicidal teens may feel helpless and alone. Most often, they also are depressed.

Allison is pregnant and scared.
The baby's father refuses to help.

He and his mother moved out of state shortly after Allison told him about the baby.

Allison can't tell her parents. They would be so disappointed in her. Allison can't bear to hurt them. She feels so hopeless and alone. In her mind, there is only one way out—suicide.

Suicide sometimes is called a permanent solution to a temporary problem. This may be true for teens who are thinking of suicide. Teens lack life experience. They haven't lived long enough to know that most problems are temporary. Teens often lack problem-solving skills that could help them cope. That is why it is important for teens who are thinking of suicide to talk with someone. No problem is so big that it can't be solved with help.

Teen suicides and adult suicides differ in some ways. Adults are more likely to complete suicide attempts. They plan more carefully. Adults tend to kill themselves because of serious illness or overwhelming problems such as debt. Loneliness following the death of a spouse or partner can be a reason for adult suicide.

Suicide Triggers

A suicide trigger is an event that causes a teen to take his or her life. Most often the teen who reacts to a suicide trigger has depression. The suicide trigger might be a divorce or death in the family. It might be one more bad event in a series of bad events. The teen might not be able to handle one more stressful situation. Common triggers for teen suicide include:

Breaking up with a boyfriend or girlfriend

Arguing with a parent

Getting a failing grade

Losing a competition

Getting blamed for something

The depressed teen might have thought about suicide for many months. The suicide trigger puts the teen over the edge.

Myth: Schools should not talk about suicide. Talking about suicide may give a teen the idea to kill himself or herself.

Fact: You don't give a suicidal person ideas by talking about suicide. The opposite is true. Discussing the subject openly can help prevent suicide.

Unrealistic Views of Death

Many reasons teens give for suicide reveal unrealistic views of death. Some teens truly do not understand how final death is. One girl said that she imagined herself dead for only a little while. A boy said that he wished only parts of him were dead.

Books and movies often show a romantic view of death. They make death seem glamorous and heroic. Teens, especially girls, may connect love with death. They may be willing to die for love.

HENRY, AGE 15

Henry is an outsider. He doesn't know why, but the other kids at school don't like him. They steal his lunch and call him names. They trip him in the hallway.

Henry feels angry and depressed. He thinks about killing himself and then fantasizes about his funeral. In his fantasy, the kids from school are standing by his grave. They are all crying and saying how sorry they are. They wish they hadn't been so mean to Henry.

Points to Consider

How does the normal process of growing up put teens at risk for suicide?

What do you do about tough situations in your life?

How do books and movies sometimes give a romanticized view of death? Give some examples from movies you have seen or books you have read.

Chapter Overview

Certain teens have a higher risk for suicide than others. Teens who are at risk may have a number of potential triggers.

A previous suicide attempt is a risk factor for a completed suicide.

Most teens who complete suicide have depression.

Risk factors for suicide include lack of self-esteem, drug and alcohol abuse, and an unstable family. Problems with sexual identity, pregnancy, or pressures to succeed also can play a role.

Chapter **3**

Who Completes Suicide?

Suicide happens among athletes, honor students, artists, and class clowns. It happens among rich kids and poor kids. It happens among kids who live in the city and kids who live in the country. Certain teens, however, may be more at risk than others.

Teens at Risk for Suicide

Teens at risk for suicide almost always have depression. They also may have more than the usual amount of stress in their life. Here are a few brief profiles. A teen might fit more than one profile.

One in six American Indian teens has attempted suicide. This is four times the rate for teens of other races and ethnic groups. American Indian teens often feel they don't fit in either white culture or American Indian culture. The feeling of not belonging anywhere is a risk factor for suicide.

Teens Who Have Attempted Suicide

Teens who have attempted suicide are at high risk for killing themselves. Between 20 and 50 percent of teens who completed suicide had made a previous attempt. A suicide attempt is like a rehearsal. It takes away some of the fear of suicide.

Teens With a Family History of Suicide

Teens with a family member who has died by suicide are at risk to take their own life. They may think suicide is an acceptable way out of their problems. Teens who cannot accept the family member's suicide may become suicidal themselves.

Suicide is not inherited. It is not a trait that a parent passes along to a child. Teens, however, may inherit a tendency toward certain mental illnesses. Mental illness is a risk factor for suicide.

Teens With Mental Illness

Teens with major depression are at risk for suicide. More than 60 percent of all people who kill themselves have major depression. People with depression have a constant feeling of sadness. For them, suicide seems like a way to end their emotional pain. Teens with bipolar disorder, panic attacks, and other mental illnesses also are at high risk for suicide. Suicide is a symptom of these illnesses as well.

Teens Who Lack Self-Esteem

Some teens have little or no self-esteem. They do not like themselves. Teens who lack self-esteem may feel worthless. They may feel they do not deserve to live. These feelings also are symptoms of depression.

Melanie hates herself. She thinks that she is ugly and fat **MELANIE, AGE 15** and that no one likes her. She tells herself she's stupid. Melanie thinks she has no talent, and she feels like she makes a fool of herself around boys. Melanie sometimes thinks about killing herself. She sits alone in her room at night holding a razor over her wrist. She imagines what it would be like to cut open her veins.

Teens Who Abuse Alcohol and Other Drugs

Between 30 and 50 percent of teen suicides occur under the influence of drugs or alcohol. Drugs and alcohol increase negative thinking and anger. They cloud a person's judgment.

Gay and Lesbian Teens

The suicide rate for gay and lesbian youth is two to six times higher than that for heterosexual youth. Almost one-third of teen suicides are committed by gay and lesbian teens. These teens may live with the daily stress of keeping their sexual identity a secret. They face many pressures that can make life painful. Teens who come out may be treated as outcasts. Gay and lesbian teens frequently endure name-calling, beatings, and other harassment.

Teens Who Experience Extreme Stress

Teens who experience an upsetting event may become extremely depressed. Their depression might lead to suicide. The divorce of parents can trigger a suicide. The death of a friend or family member also can trigger a suicide. Fear of pregnancy is a great stressor. About one-fourth of all teen girls who attempt suicide are pregnant or think they are.

Teens From Unstable Families

Mental health experts believe that family life has the greatest influence on a teen's emotional growth and happiness. Some teens experience abuse or neglect from their family. They may not have family support or a trusted family member to talk with. Teens may become suicidal because they feel unwanted and unloved. Family conflict and alcohol and drug abuse can add to feelings of hopelessness.

Gifted Teens

Teens who are talented in sports or in school may be at risk for suicide. These teens often are high achievers and very competitive. Pressure to succeed and their own unrealistic expectations may put them at risk for depression and suicide.

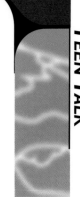
"My dad died six months ago. Nothing seems to make me happy anymore. I'm afraid I might commit suicide."
—Jamal, age 14

Ben is one of the best students in his high school class. He studies hard to keep an A average.

BEN, AGE 17

Ben could be the first person in his family to go to college. His parents, grandparents, aunts, and uncles are proud of him. His younger brothers and sisters look up to him.

Ben needs a scholarship to go to college. He did poorly on college entrance exams. Now his chances of a scholarship look dim. Ben hates himself for letting everyone down.

Points to Consider

Why would it be important to identify teens at risk for suicide?

What would you do if a friend told you she was pregnant but was afraid to tell her family?

The words to certain rock music songs seem to glorify suicide. Some people say these songs can lead young people to kill themselves. What do you think?

Chapter Overview

Untreated depression is the number one cause of teen suicide.

Depression is a medical illness. Its main symptom is an overpowering feeling of sadness. The feeling continues for a long time.

Depression is a total-body illness. It affects a person's feelings, thoughts, behavior, and physical health. It can cause a person to become suicidal.

Experts believe depression occurs when there is a chemical imbalance in the brain. The exact cause of the imbalance is unknown.

Depressed teens need professional help to get better. Treatment usually consists of medication and therapy.

Chapter **4**

Teens and Depression

It's Saturday afternoon and Luis Mendez is still in bed. His

LUIS, AGE 17

mother can't figure it out. Luis used to be an early riser, even on weekends. Mrs. Mendez knows that teens like to sleep in, but this seems extreme.

Other things bother Mrs. Mendez, too. Ever since he was a little boy, Luis has been upbeat and self-confident. Lately, he seems down on himself. He says things like, "I can't do anything right. Why do I even try?"

Luis has been skipping school. He had D's on his last report card instead of his usual A's and B's. Mrs. Mendez hopes that Luis is just going through a phase, but she's beginning to get scared.

"I felt like I was in a pitch-black tunnel. The walls were closing in on me. I was all alone."—Chantall, age 16

"I had this huge, sad feeling inside me. Nothing ever seemed to be right."—Shane, age 15

Luis shows signs of depression, which is a medical illness like cancer or heart disease. About 12 percent of teens have depression. Teens who have depression that is untreated will not necessarily take their life. However, depressed teens need prompt medical treatment to keep them from acting on suicidal urges.

Signs of Depression

Depression in teens can be difficult to diagnose, or identify. It can be hard to tell the difference between normal teenage mood swings and depression. Sometimes teens with depression become angry instead of sad. They act rebellious and hostile. Changes in mood and behavior are the most telling signs of depression or suicidal thinking or behavior.

The main symptom of depression is a feeling of deep sadness. Depression is different from normal, everyday blues. The blues usually last for a day or two. Depression goes on for more than two weeks.

The following list describes some of the most common signs of depression. A person who has five or more of these symptoms for longer than two weeks may be depressed.

Persistent sad, anxious, or "empty" mood; excessive crying; feeling of gloom

Reduced appetite and weight loss or increased appetite and weight gain

Persistent physical symptoms such as headaches, digestive disorders, and chronic, or long-lasting, pain

Irritability, restlessness

Decreased energy, fatigue, feeling "slowed down"

Feelings of guilt, worthlessness, helplessness, or hopelessness

Sleeping too much or too little, early-morning waking

Loss of interest or pleasure in activities

Difficulty concentrating, remembering, or making decisions

Thoughts of death or suicide, or suicide attempts

Myth: Anyone who tries to kill himself or herself must be crazy.

Fact: Most suicidal people are not insane. They may be depressed, upset, or full of hopelessness. Extreme distress and emotional pain are not necessarily signs of mental illness.

Effects of Depression

Depression is a total-body illness. It affects a teen's feelings, thinking, and behavior. It can affect a teen's physical health. Depression can affect all areas of a teen's life—home, school, and relationships. Teens with depression often are misunderstood. Other people may think they are lazy or unfriendly.

JAYNA AND VICKY, AGE 15

Vicky has depression. Her best friend, Jayna, knows something is wrong but doesn't know what. Vicky doesn't want to do anything anymore. The girls used to talk on the phone for hours. Now Vicky barely says hello when Jayna calls her. Jayna feels hurt. Doesn't Vicky want to be friends anymore?

Depression and Suicide

How can depression lead to suicide? Depression has a powerful effect on emotions and thoughts.

Emotional Pain

People with depression experience overpowering emotional pain. Depressed teens may try to numb their pain with drugs and alcohol. They may engage in self-harming behavior. Their pain may become so bad that they take their life to escape it.

Distorted Thinking

Depression distorts, or twists around, a person's thinking. People with depression often cannot think clearly or logically. They only are able to focus on the terrible feelings of the moment. People with depression cannot see ahead to better times. Such thinking creates feelings of hopelessness and helplessness. These feelings can lead to thoughts of suicide. Distorted thinking added to a tendency to overreact can be fatal for depressed teens.

Causes of Depression

Depression is now thought to be a disease of the brain. Like other organs in the body, the brain, too, can become sick. Research indicates that the brain of people with depression lacks certain chemicals that control mood. The exact cause of this imbalance is not known.

Some people may inherit a tendency toward depression. A stressful event may then trigger the person's depression. However, depression also develops in people with no family history of the disease. Depression can appear when things are going fine.

Depression can develop in anyone. Females, however, are twice as likely to be diagnosed with depression as males. This is one reason why females have a higher number of suicide attempts. However, females also are more likely than males to talk about their feelings and get help for their depression.

The American Association of Suicidology says to be aware of feelings. If you have any of the feelings listed below, get help. If you know someone who shows these feelings, offer help.

Can't stop the pain

Can't think clearly

Can't make decisions

Can't see any way out

Can't get out of the depression

Can't make the sadness go away

Can't see a future without pain

Can't see yourself as worthwhile

Can't get someone's attention

Can't seem to get control

Help for Depression

People with depression cannot just talk themselves into feeling good. Recovery is not a matter of willpower. People with depression need medical treatment from professionals. No one would expect people with cancer or heart disease to treat themselves. Depression requires professional help just as these other diseases do.

Treatment for depression often includes medication and psychotherapy, or talk therapy. Medications for depression are called antidepressants. They help to correct the chemical imbalance in the brain.

In psychotherapy, trained therapists meet with clients who are depressed. They talk about ways to cope with problems. Talking in a group often is helpful to depressed teens. They are able to see they are not the only ones who have the illness.

Even the blues, or temporary depression, feel bad. Here are some things you can do to chase the blues away:

Exercise.

Talk with a friend.

Do an activity you enjoy.

Volunteer at a community agency.

Play with your pet.

With proper treatment, more than 80 percent of people with depression feel better in a short time. Unfortunately, less than one-third of people with depression ever get treatment. They may not know that help is available. They may be too confused to seek help. For these people, family members and friends are important. They can learn to recognize the signs of depression and make sure the depressed person gets help.

Teens especially may need help to get treatment. If you or someone you know is depressed, talk with your parents or a school counselor. A spiritual advisor, family doctor, or other trusted adult also can provide help.

Points to Consider

Have you known someone who has been seriously depressed? If so, how did the person get help?

Do you know a teen who might be depressed? What signs do you see? What can you do to help?

Do you think you might be depressed? What signs do you see? Where can you go for help?

Why do you think females are more likely than males to have depression?

Chapter
Overview

Teens often can spot a troubled teen. They can alert responsible, caring adults who can help the teen.

Most teens who take their life give warning signs to others. These warning signs include threats of suicide and giving away prized possessions. They also include feelings of hopelessness and helplessness.

People who have made up their mind to kill themselves often appear calm and happy.

Teens who suspect a friend or family member is suicidal can do several things. They can ask the person about his or her plans, listen to problems, and tell an adult.

All suicide threats are serious. It is important to remain calm and not appear shocked.

Chapter **5**

How Can I Help My Friend?

You may be able to keep a troubled teen from taking his or her life. The teen might be your friend, brother or sister, or classmate. Teens are tuned in to other teens. You may know better than a parent what's going on with a teen. Teens are more likely to tell their problems to another teen than to a parent.

For these reasons, you may be the first to realize that a teen is suicidal. You can alert the teen's parents and other responsible adults. You can try to prevent a suicide. But remember, if the teen takes his or her life, you are not to blame.

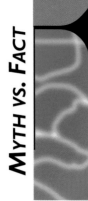

Myth: Teens in treatment won't kill themselves.

Fact: Being in treatment is no guarantee that teens won't take their life. Medications and therapy take time to be effective.

JOE, AGE 16

Joe was well liked and easygoing. He enjoyed sports and school and hanging out with his friends. Then one day Joe killed himself by jumping in front of a commuter train.

At the funeral, Joe's friends tried to make sense of it. Why had Joe done it? They had no idea he had been planning suicide.

As the boys talked, they realized there had been clues. Each friend had a piece of the puzzle. Alec remembered that Joe had just given him his prized baseball card collection. Reggie talked about the time Joe had dared him to jump from the railroad bridge into the river—then had done it himself. They all agreed that Joe had kept to himself a lot lately.

Suicide Warning Signs

Family and friends almost always express shock and disbelief at a teen suicide. They say they had no idea the teen was so troubled. The truth is, 8 out of 10 teens who kill themselves give warning signs to others.

Some of these signs are:

- Changing appearance and personality

- Giving away prized possessions

- Withdrawing from others

- Engaging in daring or risk-taking behavior

- Making comments such as, "You'd be better off without me," "What's the point of living?" or "Maybe I won't be around."

- Making direct threats such as "I feel like killing myself."

- Putting their life in order (for example, paying library fines, cleaning own room, being especially helpful)

- Having an interest in death, such as reading and asking questions about the subject

- Showing any signs of depression, especially feelings of hopelessness and helplessness

Suicidal teens may give all or only a few of the warning signs. If you know the signs, you can be alert to a teen who needs help. Troubled teens usually do not seek help on their own. You can be the one to steer a friend or family member toward safety.

The Calm Before the Storm

The most frightening warning sign might be when an unhappy, nervous teen suddenly seems calm and happy. The teen may have been struggling for months with suicidal thoughts. When suicide feels like the only choice, the teen may feel a sense of peace.

Picking Up the Signals

What should you do if you spot suicide warning signs? Find a time and place for a serious conversation with the person. Explain what you've observed. Say that you're concerned. Ask questions, listen, and then tell an adult. If the person is making suicide threats, he or she probably wants you to help.

Ask Questions

Here are several things to do when you talk to someone who may be considering suicide.

Ask key questions. Ask, "Are you thinking about killing yourself? Do you have a plan?" Be direct. You need to find out if the teen is in immediate danger. You are not putting ideas into his or her head.

Remain calm. Don't appear shocked if the teen answers yes to your questions. This could cause him or her to lose trust in you.

Take all threats of suicide seriously. You never know when and if the teen will follow through.

Don't dare the teen to take his or her life. You might think this will stop the teen, but it doesn't work in a suicide situation. Instead, it might push the teen to attempt the suicide.

Get help. If you believe the teen is in immediate danger of carrying out a suicide plan, call for help at once. You may need to call 9-1-1 or the police, or take the teen to a hospital. Do not leave the teen alone.

Listen

Suicide experts say that the best thing you can do for a suicidal person is listen. Let the person talk. You might say, "Help me understand what it's like for you" or "Tell me what's been happening." Sometimes just talking about problems makes them seem less overpowering.

Try not to offer advice or pretend to be an expert. A suicidal person doesn't want to hear what you would do. Try to get the teen to think of alternatives to suicide.

Listen, then repeat what you think the person is telling you. For example, you might say, "It sounds to me like you're not getting along with your stepfather." This is called active listening. It lets the teen know you're tuned in. The teen can correct you if you're not getting the message.

Avoid statements like "I know how you're feeling" or "Things will be better tomorrow." Without professional help, things won't get better for a depressed or suicidal person. Let the person know that you want him or her to live.

Make sure the teen knows you think the problems are serious. Don't say, "What? You're going to kill yourself because your girlfriend dumped you!" Avoid making the teen feel guilty. This only makes the person feel more helpless. Don't say, "Think how bad your mom will feel if you kill yourself." Finally, don't try to argue the teen out of suicide. The teen is not thinking logically.

Tell an Adult

The teen may try to swear you to secrecy. This is not a time to keep a secret. You must tell an adult. Let the teen know that you believe help is available. Then go together to talk with a parent, school counselor, or other trusted adult. If the teen refuses, go on your own. You may need to lose a friendship to save a life.

Shakespeare's *Romeo and Juliet* might be the most famous teen suicide. Watch the video or read the play. Then imagine that you were a friend of Romeo and Juliet. Think what you might have done to save the young lovers' life.

RAMON AND JEWEL, AGE 17

Jewel was worried about her boyfriend, Ramon. He seemed so down lately. He even talked about killing himself.

One day Jewel stopped by Ramon's house. Ramon was playing basketball at the community center. Jewel told Ramon's parents about his suicide threats. They didn't believe he was serious.

"He's just trying to get your attention," Ramon's dad said. "He's just going through a phase," sighed his mom.

Jewel wasn't so sure. The next day she talked with the youth director at the community center. She knew that Ramon liked and respected him. The director said he'd help Ramon get into counseling.

Points to Consider

What would you do if a friend or family member seemed to be joking about killing himself or herself?

Do you know anyone who shows suicide warning signs? What can you do about it?

Why do you think adults often overlook suicide warning signs in teens?

Chapter
Overview

Knowing what to do during a suicide attempt can save a person's life.

Most suicidal people decide to carry out the act on impulse. If the person can be helped through the crisis, the impulse to commit suicide often passes. However, treatment is needed to prevent another crisis.

Suicide prevention hot lines can provide help in a crisis. Trained volunteers help suicidal callers find other ways to resolve problems.

Teens who have attempted suicide are desperately unhappy. They need professional help to cope with the problems in their life.

Teens who have attempted suicide need the support of family and friends more than ever.

Chapter **6**

What to Do in a Crisis

The phone rang. Darcy
picked it up and heard the
voice of her friend Jo.

DARCY AND JO, AGE 15

"Darcy, help me," Jo said. Her words were soft and slurred.

"What? I can hardly hear you," Darcy replied. Her heart
started beating faster. She could feel an awful knot forming in
her stomach.

"I took some of Mom's sleeping pills. I don't want to die . . . ."
Jo's voice trailed off.

If someone you know is in real danger of suicide, you must act at
once. In some cases, the person already has made the attempt.
Knowing what to do can save the person's life.

How to Handle an Emergency

Remain calm during a suicide attempt. If you become panicky, your friend likely will panic, too.

If your friend has called you, try to keep the person on the phone. Find out where your friend is. If someone else is with you, have that person find another phone and call 9-1-1. If you are alone, tell your friend you will call right back. Hang up and call for help.

If you are alone with a friend threatening suicide, call for adult help. If it is safe to do so, remove guns, ropes, knives, pills, or anything else the teen might use. You may need to call 9-1-1. Stay until help arrives. Never leave a suicidal person alone.

Suicidal people may have thought for months about killing themselves. Even so, the actual act often is impulsive, especially with teens. The suicidal crisis usually lasts only about 15 minutes. Keeping your friend from acting for that long may be enough to save his or her life. Encourage the person to talk about the situation. Use the listening skills described in chapter 5.

Here are some hot line numbers you can call for immediate help or advice. It does not cost money to call these numbers.

Covenant House Nineline (24 hours)	1-800-999-9999
National Boys Town Hotline (24 hours) (Girls can call this hot line, too.)	1-800-448-3000
National Child Abuse Hotline (24 hours)	1-800-4-A-CHILD (800-422-4453)
National Suicide Hotline	1-800-SUICIDE (800-784-2433)

You might try to get the person to agree not to do anything until you've talked. Sometimes just knowing that another person cares is enough to pull the teen through the crisis. Contact your friend's parents or caregivers right away.

Suicide Prevention Hot Lines

Suicide prevention hot lines can save lives. You can call these special telephone numbers to get immediate help or advice for your friend. You might say, "I'm with someone who is thinking about suicide. Please tell us what to do."

Trained volunteers answer suicide hot lines 24 hours a day. They help suicidal callers talk about their feelings and think of reasons to live. They also tell callers how to find more help.

Your local suicide hot line number should be listed on the inside front cover of your telephone book or under *Suicide Intervention*. Some hot lines are especially for teens. You also might call the toll-free national crisis numbers listed on this page.

"As I hit the water, I suddenly realized I wanted to live. I prayed that someone had seen me jump."
—Mack, age 17, rescued by water patrol after suicide attempt

If You Feel Suicidal

You may be the one who feels suicidal. It is critical to get help right away. Take the following steps:

Wait. The suicidal impulse usually passes once you get through the crisis.

Don't cut off yourself from others. Depression feeds on loneliness. Talk with someone you trust. Let someone who can help know how you're feeling.

If you don't want to speak with someone you know, call a suicide prevention hot line. Your call will be confidential.

Remember that suicide is a permanent solution to a temporary problem.

After the Crisis

Once the crisis has passed, the person needs follow-up help. The person may be hospitalized. Doctors may prescribe medications. Therapy can help the person find ways to deal with problems and stress. After leaving the hospital, the person will continue treatment as an outpatient.

Myth: If a person is determined to die by suicide, nothing is going to stop him or her.

Fact: Even the most depressed people have mixed feelings about death. They go back and forth until the last moment. They want to live and they want to die. However, most suicidal people do not really want death. They want the pain to stop. The urge to end their life does not last forever.

Teens who have attempted suicide need the love and support of family and friends. They may feel embarrassed. They may not want to talk about the suicide attempt. You can let the person know that you are available to listen. Your concern may give the person confidence to open up. Talking can provide a great deal of relief for everyone.

Points to Consider

Why do you think a suicidal crisis lasts such a short period of time? List three things you could do to help in a crisis.

Whom would you talk with or call if you felt suicidal? Why would you choose this person?

How could you help a teen who has returned to school after a suicide attempt? Why might this teen have a hard time?

Chapter Overview

People often think of suicide as something shameful. This attitude makes it difficult for people struggling with suicidal thoughts to get help.

Suicide is a health issue. It must be brought into the open and talked about.

More and more schools have suicide prevention programs.

Local and national groups are working to educate the public about suicide and ways to prevent it.

The media can play a part in educating the public about suicide prevention.

Changes in society could help reduce the rising number of teen suicides.

Chapter **7**

Suicide Prevention

Imagine 5,000 teens dying each year of the measles. People would be outraged. They would call for immediate action. In its own way, teen suicide is like a widespread disease. People need to be angry about this waste of life. Much can be done to prevent teens from killing themselves.

Suicide and Secrecy

Secrecy often surrounds suicide in the United States and Canada. Relatives and friends may keep the suicide of a loved one a secret, or they may talk about it only in private. To them, suicide is shameful. They may believe that anyone who commits suicide is weak and cowardly.

Cal ran a hose from the tailpipe of the family car into the backseat. He closed the garage door and the car windows. Then he got into the car and started the engine. In a short while, Cal was dead from breathing carbon monoxide, a deadly gas.

CAL, AGE 16

Cal's parents refused to acknowledge that Cal had killed himself. They felt ashamed. No one in their family had ever died by suicide. They worried that people would think they were bad parents. Cal's parents told everyone that he had died from an unknown cause.

Suicide is the most preventable death. One important way to prevent suicide is to talk about it openly. People need to know that suicide is a health issue. A person who feels suicidal need not feel ashamed to seek help. Families and friends of those who kill themselves need not feel ashamed to seek help, either.

Suicide Prevention Programs for Teens

Many schools in the United States and Canada have programs to prevent teen suicide. Some schools train teachers to spot depressed and suicidal students. Teachers also learn to be aware of suicidal themes in student drawings, poetry, or essays.

Much of the shame surrounding suicide stems from long-ago traditions. During the Middle Ages, many Europeans thought people who killed themselves were murderers. Their body might be burned, dragged through the street, or tossed in the dump. The family of suicide victims also was punished.

Other schools have peer support or peer counseling programs. These programs teach students to recognize suicide warning signals in their classmates. Students learn how to listen to a troubled teen. They learn what to do in an emergency. Teens often find it easier to accept help from someone their own age.

Suicide prevention is part of health classes in many schools. Many schools are attempting to reach out to students who are treated as outcasts.

Educating the Public

The American Association of Suicidology and other groups educate the public about teen suicide. These groups publish information and provide speakers for school and community groups. They help set up suicide prevention programs. They also provide services to families who have lost a teen to suicide.

Mara waited for a city bus after school. It was cold and windy, so she stepped inside the bus shelter.

MARA, AGE 15

A poster on the wall of the shelter caught Mara's eye. The girl in the poster looked a lot like Mara—dark hair, dark eyes, shy smile. Above her picture were the words "Suicide's number one cause is untreated depression."

Mara felt the poster was speaking to her. She had been depressed for a long time. Thoughts of suicide had crossed her mind.

The poster had the number of a suicide prevention hot line. Mara copied it down in her notebook. Maybe someone at the hot line could tell her what to do to feel better.

Suicide and the Media

Newspapers, television, and other media can help to prevent teen suicide. Programs about suicides often list phone numbers of suicide prevention hot lines and the names of counseling centers. These programs may talk about symptoms and signs and suggest treatment. They can help reduce the shame of depression and suicide.

Suicide claims about 30,000 lives in the United States each year. It is the eighth-leading cause of death. Today, another 83 Americans will kill themselves.

Improving Society

Improvements in society also could prevent teen suicide. Lawmakers could pass laws to make it more difficult for teens to get guns. Laws requiring barriers on observation decks and bridges could discourage suicide attempts. Building strong families and ending violence and drug abuse could reduce factors that contribute to teen suicide.

Points to Consider

If someone in your family died by suicide, would you talk about it? Why or why not?

What efforts has your school made toward suicide prevention?

What can you do to help support suicide prevention?

Chapter
Overview

Suicide survivors are people who have lost a loved one to suicide. They must face the normal grief of losing someone to death. They also struggle to understand why it happened.

Suicide survivors experience many painful emotions. Although the pain may lessen with time, it never goes away entirely.

Grief counselors and suicide support groups can help survivors come to terms with their loss.

Suicide survivors are never to blame for someone's suicide.

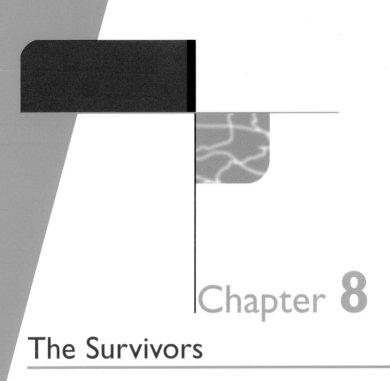

Chapter **8**

The Survivors

A teen's suicide deeply affects many people. Family, friends, and others are left to grieve and to wonder why. The people left behind after a suicide are suicide survivors. Their life will never be the same.

A suicide survivor is a person who was close to someone who committed suicide. At least 4.4 million people in the United States today are survivors of a loved one's suicide.

DEREK, AGE 18

Derek's brother, Randy, hanged himself 10 years ago. Randy's death hit Derek hard. He had idolized his older brother and tagged along wherever he went.

For years, Derek blamed himself for Randy's death. The two brothers had argued shortly before Randy died. Therapy helped Derek realize that Randy's depression caused his suicide. It wasn't Derek's fault.

Randy's death haunted Derek all through high school. Derek thought people wondered if he, too, would kill himself someday. Derek's parents constantly watched him. Derek wished he could be a normal kid with normal emotions.

Derek's grief and anger have subsided, but a certain sadness lingers on. This year was particularly hard for Derek. He graduated from high school, and he wanted Randy to be there. Sometimes he says to Randy, "See what you and I missed?"

Powerful Emotions

Suicide survivors may experience some or all of the following strong emotions:

Shock. Shock may be the first reaction. Survivors feel numb. They cannot believe that the suicide happened. Shock is useful. It allows the brain to absorb the horrible news slowly.

Sorrow. Survivors feel great sadness. Some may cry and sob. Others will scream and wail. Still others may be silent.

Guilt. Survivors frequently blame themselves. They keep saying, "If only I had . . . , she would be alive today." They wonder if they said or did something to cause the suicide. Survivors may feel guilty because they are alive and the person is dead.

Anger. Suicide survivors often look for someone or something to blame. They feel anger toward themselves or others for not stopping the suicide. They feel anger toward the person who died for not asking for help. Survivors may feel deserted or rejected.

Relief. The person may have had a long battle with depression or other illness. Survivors may feel relief that the person's struggle is over. Such feelings of relief can make survivors feel even more guilty.

Depression. Survivors may fall into a deep depression. They may need medication and therapy to get better.

Suicidal urges. The emotional pain of suicide may cause survivors to feel suicidal. The suicide rate for survivors is eight times higher than the suicide rate for the general public.

Physical Symptoms
Suicide survivors may have physical symptoms such as headaches. They may have trouble sleeping or feel constantly anxious. These symptoms are a response to their grief. Sometimes survivors treat their physical symptoms and avoid the emotions that cause them.

If You Are a Suicide Survivor
You may be the brother, sister, or friend of a teen who died by suicide. You are a suicide survivor. You know better than anyone that life following a suicide is difficult.

"My support group helped me the most. These people felt the same way I did. I could say anything to them and know they understood."
—Andrea, age 17, suicide survivor

Dealing With Your Emotions

It is all right to feel sad, angry, guilty, and other emotions. You have had a shocking loss. You need to accept your emotions and release them. It is dangerous and unhealthy to keep your emotions bottled up inside you.

Talking about your feelings can help. You might talk with a spiritual advisor, school counselor, or other trusted adult. If possible, talk with someone trained in grief counseling. Support groups for suicide survivors can connect you with others who know what you're going through. The Useful Addresses and Internet Sites section in the back of this book lists organizations that can help you.

You Are Not to Blame

Here is an important reminder. You are not responsible for another person's suicide. You cannot control the thoughts and actions of others just as no one can control your thoughts and actions.

"My advice to anyone who has been through a suicide is to talk, talk, talk."—Darrin, age 15, suicide survivor

More Ways to Cope

Here are more ways to cope with the suicide of a teen who was important to you.

Take care of yourself. You can cope with your emotions better if you're in good health. Eat balanced meals and exercise regularly. Get enough sleep. Find activities and hobbies you enjoy doing.

Be open to new friendships and activities. You may feel disloyal if you make new friends or go out and have fun. This way of thinking doesn't help you. Reaching out to others will help you heal. You always can keep the person in your heart and mind.

Use your anger constructively. You may be mad that the person left you. Do something positive with your anger. Do good deeds for others.

Speak out about suicide. Tell others the facts about teen suicide.

If You Know a Suicide Survivor

You may not have been close to a teen who died by suicide. However, you may know someone who is a survivor. Here are some ways to help that person.

Don't avoid the survivor. Send a note, say hello, or call on the phone. You might invite the person to do something with you.

Listen. Let the person talk about his or her feelings. You don't need to offer advice. Just having someone listen can help the person work through his or her grief.

Provide practical help. Suicide survivors often feel confused for a time. They may be unable to focus on daily activities. You can help by running errands, baby-sitting, and much more.

Write a letter. Include your favorite memories of the teen who died. Tell why you'll miss the person.

Every 100 minutes a person under the age of 25 completes suicide.

Students at Jefferson High School were stunned. Two of

JEFFERSON HIGH SCHOOL

their classmates, a popular girl and boy, had killed themselves.

The day after the suicides, the principal called an all-school assembly. He wanted to discuss the suicides openly and allow the students to ask questions. The principal told the facts of the deaths. He asked the students to think about other choices the teens might have made. He was careful not to make the teens seem brave or noble.

After the assembly, students could go to "safe" rooms to talk privately with mental health counselors. The school also sent letters to all the parents listing the warning signs of suicide. The quick response of Jefferson's principal and staff helped the students begin to heal.

Points to Consider

How have schools in your community tried to help students cope with the death of a classmate?

Should a teen's suicide be mentioned at the funeral or in funeral notices? Why or why not?

Do you know anyone who is a suicide survivor? How can you help this person?

Glossary

antidepressant (an-teye-di-PRESS-uhnt)—a drug used to relieve the symptoms of depression

bipolar disorder (beye-POH-lur di-SOR-dur)—a type of mood disorder in which a person has extreme mood swings; the person goes from feeling very low (depression) to feeling very high (mania).

blues (blooz)—having low spirits; temporary depression.

carbon monoxide (KAR-buhn muh-NOK-side)—a poisonous gas produced by the engines of vehicles

diagnose (dye-ugh-NOHSS)—to determine an illness

dysthymia (diss-THY-mee-uh)—a mild but long-lasting form of depression

distort (diss-TORT)—to twist around; to change the facts.

fantasy (FAN-tuh-see)—an imagined happening; something that is not likely to happen in real life.

fatal (FAY-tuhl)—deadly

impulsive (im-PUHL-siv)—tending to act without thinking

inherited (in-HER-it-ed)—a trait passed down from a parent to a child

psychiatrist (sye-KYE-uh-trist)—a medical doctor who specializes in the diagnosis and treatment of mental illness

psychologist (sye-KOL-uh-jist)—a mental health professional who specializes in diagnosing and treating mental illness; a psychologist treats people mainly through conversation.

psychotherapy (sye-koh-THER-uh-pee)—a type of treatment for depression in which a therapist attempts to help a person through conversation

romantic (roh-MAN-tic)—an adventurous or heroic idea that is not realistic or practical

For More Information

Cobain, Bev. *When Nothing Matters Anymore: A Survival Guide for Depressed Teens.* Minneapolis: Free Spirit, 1998.

Goldman, Nikki M. *Teenage Suicide.* New York: Benchmark Books, 1996.

Mitchell, Hayley R. *Teen Suicide.* San Diego: Lucent, 2000.

Peacock, Judith. *Depression.* Mankato, MN: Capstone Press, 2000.

Woog, Adam. *Suicide.* San Diego: Lucent, 1997.

Useful Addresses and Internet Sites

American Association of Suicidology
4201 Connecticut Avenue Northwest
Suite 408
Washington, DC 20008
www.suicidology.org

American Psychiatric Association
1400 K Street Northwest, Suite 501
Washington, DC 20005
www.psych.org

Canadian Mental Health Association
2160 Yonge Street, 3rd Floor
Toronto, Ontario M4S 2Z3
CANADA
www.cmha.ca

National Alliance for the Mentally Ill
200 North Glebe Road, Suite 1015
Arlington, VA 22203-3754
1-800-950-6264 (NAMI Helpline)
www.nami.org

National Depressive and Manic-Depressive
Association
730 North Franklin Street, Suite 501
Chicago, IL 60610-3526
1-800-82-NDMDA (800-826-3632)
www.ndmda.org

National Mental Health Association
1021 Prince Street
Alexandria, VA 22314-2971
1-800-969-NMHA (800-969-6642)
www.nmha.org

Covenant House
www.covenanthouse.org
Provides information about teen problems,
including suicide
Covenant House Nineline
1-800-999-9999

Depression.com
www.depression.com
News articles and information about depression
and medications prescribed for depression

Make a Noise
www.makeanoise.ysp.org.au
Information about mental health, physical
health, drug prevention, and more

Reach Out
www.reachout.asn.au
Suicide prevention resources for teens

Suicide Awareness\Voices of Education
(SA\VE)
www.save.org
Facts about suicide and depression and
information about suicide prevention

DEPRESSION/Awareness, Recognition, and
Treatment Program (D/ART)
1-800-421-4211

Index

Index continued